FORESTS FOR THE FUTURE

Edward Parker

RSVP

RAINTREE
STECK-VAUGHN
P U B L I S H E R S

The Steck-Vaughn Company

Austin, Texas

PROTECTING OUR PLANET

FORESTS FOR THE FUTURE

FUELS FOR THE FUTURE

KEEPING THE AIR CLEAN

KEEPING WATER CLEAN

PROTECTING WILD PLACES

WASTE, RECYCLING AND RE-USE

Published by Raintree Steck-Vaughn Publishers, an imprint of Steck-Vaughn Company

Library of Congress Cataloging-in-Publication Data
Parker, Edward.
Forests for the future / Edward Parker.
     p.   cm.—(Protecting our planet)
     Includes bibliographical references and index.
     Summary: Describes northern, temperate, and tropical forests, the problems of preserving them, and their future prospects.
     ISBN 0-8172-4934-6
     1. Forests and forestry—Juvenile literature.
     2. Forest conservation—Juvenile literature.
     3. Forest ecology—Juvenile literature.
     4. Deforestation—Juvenile literature.
     [1. Forests and forestry. 2. Forest conservation.]
     I. Title. II. Series.
     SD376.P37   1998
     333.75—dc21   97-1258

Printed in Italy. Bound in the United States.
1 2 3 4 5 6 7 8 9 0 02 01 00 99 98

CONTENTS

INTRODUCTION 4

THE WORLD'S FORESTS 6

FORESTS AND THE WORLD ENVIRONMENT 10

FORESTS AND HUMAN LIFE 16

DISAPPEARING FORESTS 24

WHAT IS BEING DONE? 34

FORESTS FOR THE FUTURE 44

GLOSSARY 46

FURTHER INFORMATION 47

INDEX 48

INTRODUCTION

Forests form some of the most spectacular and important ecosystems on earth, providing habitats for millions of animal and plant species. They are also home to millions of indigenous people around the world who depend on them directly for food, shelter, fuel, and medicines.

We do not, however, need to live in or near the world's great forests to benefit from them. Almost every aspect of our daily lives, even in cities, is linked to forests. The oxygen we breathe is regulated by forests. The water we drink is recycled by trees, and tropical rain forests help maintain our global climate. Many of our most popular foods, such as chocolate, bananas, and coffee, originated in forests. Even fish sticks are held together using wood pulp from trees!

▼ A hunter from New Guinea returns from the forest with a European pig. These animals were introduced in the seventeenth century by passing traders.

■ Forest areas

▲ Forests cover almost one-third of the earth's surface.

▲ A tug pulls a huge floating boom of logs to a saw mill in Skagit Bay, in Washington State.

Forests have provided essential resources for the great civilizations of the past. Today, they provide the industrial world with many of the raw materials needed for multibillion dollar industries. These materials include timber, wood pulp, gums, resins, nuts, fruits, and medicinal plants. Products from trees are used for a huge range of consumer goods from cancer drugs to eyeglass frames, aircraft tires, and car paints. Every time we read a book or magazine or use photographic film to take a picture, we use wood pulp from forest trees.

Forests cover around 30 percent of the earth's land surface. They are centers of great biological richness, containing more than 70 percent of the world's land-living plant and animal species. But they are disappearing at an alarming rate. Large areas of tropical rain forest have already been cut down, and much of the ancient temperate rain forest in North America and Chile is due to be clear-cut in the next ten years. Forests are vital to life on earth, and they are a resource that must be managed wisely.

TREE FACTS

● The oldest living organism on earth today is the bristlecone pine, which can live for more than 5,000 years. That is equivalent to 200 human generations.

● California redwood trees can weigh up to 6,000 tons, making them the largest living organisms on the planet.

● Some of the trees in temperate forests of northwest America can grow to over 325 ft. (100 m) tall, and are the biggest living organisms alive today. Even bigger were the monkey thorn trees of South Africa's Transvaal. They reached a staggering 400 ft. (120 m) tall and 150 ft. (45 m) around the trunk, but they had all been cut down by the beginning of this century.

● A 200-year-old arctic willow may have a trunk only about as thick as a human finger.

THE WORLD'S FORESTS

Trees have existed on the earth for around 275 million years, and for 90 million years they dominated the earth's vegetation. During this period—known as the Carboniferous Era—millions of tons of plant material were laid down and later compressed under sediments over a long time, to form the fossil fuels such as coal, oil, and gas that we depend on today.

During their long history many types of trees and forests have evolved. Today there are thousands of different tree species growing in a great variety of forest types—from tropical rain forests and coastal mangrove forests to subarctic pine forests.

HUMAN INFLUENCE

Forests throughout the world have been changed by people. Where a forest has been relatively undisturbed by human activity, it is called **primary** forest. Where people have had a significant effect and the original forest has been greatly altered, it is known as **secondary** forest. A **plantation** is an artificial forest where tree species have been planted to provide a particular product, such as timber.

▶ Temperate pine forests in Baker National Park, in Washington State.

Trees can be divided into two broad types: conifers and broadleaved trees. Conifer literally means "cone bearing," and these trees are typically evergreen and often have needle-shaped leaves. Broadleaved trees are often deciduous (losing their leaves seasonally) and have a wide variety of leaf shapes.

The world's forests are generally divided into three main types. These are boreal, or northern forests; temperate forests; and tropical forests. However, there is not usually any clear line to show where one forest type ends and another begins. The situation is also complicated by altitude, since highland areas in temperate or tropical forests can contain trees that are usually found only in much cooler locations.

Boreal forest
Temperate forest
Tropical forest

▲ The most common types of forest are shown in the shaded areas.

BOREAL FORESTS

The boreal forests stretch across Russia, Norway, Finland, Sweden, the United States, and Canada, forming an almost continuous belt around the earth. Although they are generally found between the latitudes 45°–60° North, some Siberian forests are situated as far north as 70°. Together, these forests make up one of the world's last great wildernesses that, until recently, had been little altered by human activity.

Boreal forests are characterized by hot summers, extremely cold winters, and low rainfall. The result of this harsh climate is a growing season of only three months each year, which is too short for most types of trees. Only hardy conifers such as spruce, larch, fir, and pine trees thrive in these conditions, although it can take a tree 150–200 years to reach maturity.

▲ Boreal forests consist mainly of slow-growing needleleaf trees such as larch.

TEMPERATE FORESTS

There are many types of temperate forests, and they occur in both the Northern and Southern hemispheres. The word "temperate" means moderate, and this describes the weather conditions that are found in the parts of the world where these forests grow: Warm summers, mild winters, and high rainfall are spread evenly throughout the year. These conditions are ideal for both conifers and broadleaved trees.

Temperate rain forest grows along the northwest coast of North America. Although it is dominated by conifer tree species, such as Sitka spruce and Douglas fir, it is quite unlike the conifer forests of the boreal region. North America's temperate rain forests are home to some of the oldest and largest trees on earth. Douglas fir trees, for example, can be up to 300 ft. (90 m) high and 16 ft. (5 m) in diameter.

In other temperate areas, forests are generally made up of a mixture of broadleaved trees and conifers. In Great Britain, for example, forests and woodlands range from those dominated by oak and beech in the lowlands, to birch and pine forests in the uplands.

▲ Temperate forests consist of a complex mix of broadleaf and needleleaf trees. They are home to the largest trees, such as Hemlock and Giant Redwood.

▼ Mosses thrive on living and dead trees in the moist and mild climate of a temperate rain forest.

▲ About half the world's tropical forests are dry like this one in the northwestern Transvaal, South Africa.

TROPICAL FORESTS

Located between the tropics of Cancer and Capricorn, tropical forests cover approximately 14 percent of the earth's land surface. There are two main types: tropical rain forests and tropical dry forests.

Tropical rain forests are the most complex and diverse ecosystems on earth, and scientists have estimated that they could contain between 50 and 90 percent of the world's plant and animal species. For example, in one 125-acre (50-ha) plot of tropical rain forest in Malaysia, 835 tree species have been identified.

Tropical rain forests are found in hot and humid conditions, where the average temperature during the coldest month of the year is no lower than 65° F (18° C) and there is at least 4 in. (100 mm) of rain every month.

In contrast to the dense, luxuriant tropical rain forest, tropical dry forests often have trees that are widely scattered and are usually small and scrubby in appearance. They tend to grow in areas where the climate is hot and dry, and the trees may lose their leaves during the driest months. While these dry forests do not contain as many species as rain forests, they are the habitat for some of the world's most magnificent animals such as elephants, rhinos, and lions.

▲Tropical forests tend to contain a wide variety of broadleaf evergreen trees like the one shown here.

9

FORESTS AND THE WORLD ENVIRONMENT

Forests are valuable for many reasons. The timber, foods, and medicines that use ingredients from forests are worth billions of dollars every year. However, they are also extremely valuable to us in ways that are difficult to calculate in terms of money.

These children in the Philippines were orphaned and made homeless by flash floods. This happened because the forests on surrounding hills had been cut down, increasing the amount of water flowing down hillsides.

FLOODS AND DROUGHT

Trees play an extremely important role in the control of floods and droughts. During torrential rains the leaves in the forest canopy break the fall of raindrops, reducing their impact on the soil and young plants below. The spaces in the soil made by tree roots then help the water to soak in. Forests work like huge sponges soaking up rainfall and releasing it slowly throughout the year into streams and topping off underground water supplies.

Land covered with trees and other plants absorbs 20 times as much rainwater as bare earth. Where forests have been removed, the rainwater flows over the surface of the land causing floods. And because only a small proportion of the rainwater soaks into the ground there is often too little left for the rest of the year.

▲ Rain falling over the rain-forested foothills of the Bolivian Andes.

A PHILIPPINE DISASTER

In November 1991 flash floods raced down the hillsides above the coastal town of Ormoc in the Philippines. Within minutes the water rose to 13 ft. (4 m) deep in the streets. Seven thousand people were drowned.

The tragedy was blamed on illegal logging, which had stripped the hills of the dense rain forest that once clothed them. Without the forests to absorb it, the torrential tropical rain raced down valleys, smashing houses and bursting riverbanks. Thousands of illegally cut logs were swept down from the mountainsides, giving a clue to the cause of the disaster.

Ninety years ago 80 percent of the Philippines was covered with forest. Now it has fewer trees per person than any other Southeast Asian country, mostly because of illegal logging.

PHILIPPINES

Manila ●

● Ormoc

India is a good example of how the cutting down of forests causes floods and droughts. About 150 million acres (60 million ha) of land in India are now vulnerable to flooding: more than twice as much as 30 years ago. And in the Indian state of Uttar Pradesh alone —where there has been heavy logging activity—the number of villages that are short of water has risen from 17,000 to 70,000 in the last twenty years.

▼ This diagram shows the effects of deforestation. Tree loss leads to soil erosion and landslides. These are often followed by the silting up of rivers and reservoirs, which shortens the life of dams and causes flooding.

Reservoirs become silted up

Soil raises water level, flooding homes and fields

Trees cut

Soil erosion

Landslides

Crops lost

Silt forms new islands, blocking estuaries and damaging coastal fisheries

WILDLIFE AND BIODIVERSITY

Forests in all their forms provide habitats for more than 70 percent of all land-living species on the planet. Rain forests provide the most dramatic example, containing over half of all terrestrial species but covering only 6 percent of the earth's land surface. In a typical 2,500-acre (1,000-ha) patch of rain forest, biologists would expect to find 1,500 species of flowering plants, 750 kinds of trees, 400 bird species, and more than 150 kinds of butterflies. A forest on one volcano in the Philippines has more plant species than the entire United States! Forests even influence sea life—70 percent of all fish caught throughout the world hatch in coastal mangroves and estuaries.

A pigtailed macaque in the forests of Borneo

MANGROVES—FORESTS WITH THEIR FEET IN THE SEA

Mangroves are a special type of rain forest that line one-quarter of the world's tropical coastlines. The 55 different types of mangrove cover an area of approximately 925 sq. mi. (2,400 sq. km).

The trees are readily identifiable because of their bell-shaped root systems that lift the trunk above the mud and water. These "breathing" roots enable mangroves to survive in areas of very salty water, usually along coastlines, or in water with reduced oxygen, for example in swamps.

Mangrove forests give coastlines vital protection from the destructive effects of storm-force winds and waves. They also provide a sheltered environment and the clean, silt-free water that thousands of aquatic species need to breed in. More than 2,000 species of fish and invertebrates (for example, shrimp) are believed to use mangroves as spawning grounds.

Mangroves provide important resources for people who live along tropical coasts. These forests have been shown to be as productive as farmlands, providing shellfish, shrimp, crabs, fish, and firewood for millions of people around the world.

▲ Many ocean fish and crustaceans breed in the mangrove forest because they can find protection from predators among the roots of the trees.

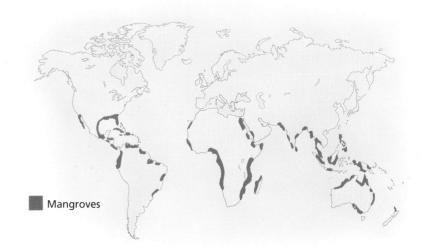

■ Mangroves

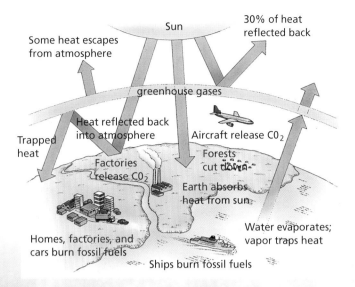

Sun

30% of heat reflected back

Some heat escapes from atmosphere

greenhouse gases

Heat reflected back into atmosphere

Trapped heat

Aircraft release CO_2

Factories release CO_2

Forests cut down

Earth absorbs heat from sun

Homes, factories, and cars burn fossil fuels

Water evaporates; vapor traps heat

Ships burn fossil fuels

GLOBAL WARMING

Scientific evidence has recently shown that the earth is warming up. This has been caused mainly by an increase in the proportion of carbon dioxide gas in the atmosphere. Presently, carbon dioxide in the atmosphere rises by 1 percent each year. If this trend continues, the world will experience a temperature rise of 5° F (3° C) by the year 2100, making the earth warmer than at any time during the last 100,000 years. To give an idea of how serious this is, a rise of 7° F (4° C) would mean that the earth would be exposed to temperatures not experienced since 40 million years ago.

As trees grow they absorb carbon dioxide from the air. Together the world's trees and soils contain two billion tons of carbon. This is locked up in complex chemicals, such as fats and proteins, found in living and dead organic material. However, when organic matter such as wood decomposes or is burned, it releases most of its stored carbon into the atmosphere as carbon dioxide gas. Cutting down forests has produced half of all man-made emissions over the last 130 years. The other half has come from burning fossil fuels such as coal, oil, and gas, which are the compressed remains of plants that grew millions of years ago.

▼ Forests absorb the energy from the sun by transpiring—releasing water vapor through pores in the leaves. This helps make the local climate in tropical forest areas cooler.

Scientists have proposed planting trees as a way of collecting and storing carbon to help counteract the buildup of carbon dioxide. Their research has shown that while fast-growing plantation trees could help, protecting "old growth" forests is a much more efficient way of storing carbon. Each year 16 percent of atmospheric carbon dioxide is cycled through plants, and forests contain up to 85 percent of all carbon that is bound up in living organisms.

CLIMATE

The weather in forested regions is generally milder, moister, and less variable than in treeless regions. The boreal forests, for example, warm the subarctic region by providing a dark mass capable of absorbing heat from the sun. Trees in hot areas, on the other hand, have a cooling effect.

Forests also affect the amount of rain that falls on them. Trees pump up vast quantities of water from the ground. This water evaporates from the leaves, releasing moisture into the air. The moisture gathers as clouds and then falls as rain again. At least half of the rain that falls on the Amazon is recycled in this way.

Where the rain forest has been cut down in Madagascar large quantities of soil have been washed away, sometimes leaving just bare rock.

SOIL LOSS

Trees catch much of the rain falling onto a forest, softening its destructive power before it reaches the ground. Tree roots create spaces for the water to soak away and help bind the soil. When trees are removed, especially from mountainsides, the soil is soon washed away by rain. A recent study in Ivory Coast in Africa has shown that a deforested hill loses 500 times as much soil as one covered with trees. Forest destruction around the world causes the loss of 50 billion tons of topsoil every year.

Soil erosion is now so severe that it can be seen from space. Astronauts have commented that the African island of Madagascar looks as if it is bleeding to death because of the millions of tons of red topsoil washed into the Indian Ocean from the deforested hillsides.

FORESTS AND HUMAN LIFE

Wooden houses being built in New Zealand. They are safer in areas where there is threat of earthquakes because the frames are more flexible than steel and concrete.

Forests have been vitally important to humans throughout our history. The prehistoric origins of many religions are linked to trees, and the importance of forests and trees themselves lives on in ancient customs. Belief in a "Tree of Life" that links heaven, earth, and the underworld is a very ancient one, and this symbol appears in myths from the Arctic to Australia.

Throughout history people have relied on trees for fuel, tools, and building materials. The societies of Mycenae and Minoan Crete—which existed between 4,500 and 3,200 year ago—used 120 pine trees to smelt every ingot of bronze. However, in the fourth century B.C. the Greek philosopher Plato was already writing about the deforested hills around Athens, noting that "what now remains is like the skeleton of a sick man." After cutting down most of the forests near Rome the Romans were forced to expand their empire in order to secure vital supplies of wood.

War had a particularly severe effect on the forests of Europe in the Middle Ages and later. For example, more than a quarter of a million trees were cut down to build the Christian and Turkish fleets that fought at the Battle of Lepanto in 1571. By the eighteenth century, it took 2,000 large trees to make a single warship.

▲ A painting depicting the wooden galleons of the Spanish Armada at sea

The Industrial Revolution, which began in Europe around the mid-eighteenth century, was powered by coal—the fossilized remains of trees that died millions of years ago.

FOREST PEOPLE

More than 140 million people live in or around forests and rely directly on them. For example, half the world's population uses wood as a fuel for cooking and heating. While an increasing proportion of the people who now live in forests are relative newcomers, about 1–2.5 million indigenous people have been living in them for many thousands of years. For these people, forests have traditionally provided everything, including their spiritual and cultural identity.

Indigenous people have developed a great understanding of the nature of the forests in which they live. Many know of practical uses for almost all the trees in their traditional areas—for foods, medicines, hunting, fishing, or building materials, or for their spiritual needs.

▲ A Penan man from the rain forest hunting with a hardwood blowpipe, on the rain forest island of Sarawak

A Nenets reindeer herder bends the larch runners of a new sled into shape.

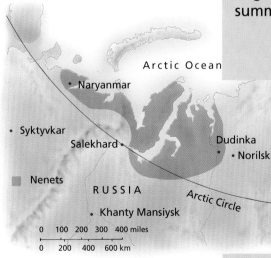

Arctic Ocean

• Naryanmar

• Syktyvkar

Salekhard •

Dudinka
•

• Norilsk

Nenets

RUSSIA

Arctic Circle

• Khanty Mansiysk

0   100 200 300 400 miles

0   200   400   600 km

A NENETS MAKES A SLED

One of the native peoples in northern Siberia is a group of reindeer herders known as the Nenets. Each spring they migrate 600 mi. (1,000 km) with their reindeer herds to the summer pastures in the north of the Yamal Peninsula. They head south each autumn to winter over in the forests just south of the Arctic Circle. Each group of herders is made up of several families and up to 4,000 reindeer.

The Nenets make their sleds in a way that has changed little over the last thousand years. They use larch wood from the Siberian forest known as the taiga. It takes several days to make each sled, which usually requires wood from three larch trees. The runners are made by steaming and gently bending them into shape over heat. The whole construction is held together by wooden pegs.

Indigenous people live not only in tropical rain forests but also in many other forest areas around the world. For example, the temperate rain forests of Alaska are the ancestral home of the Tlinglit and other traditional peoples; Aborigine groups live in the forests of northern Australia; while the Mahgreb are Berber people who live in the Atlas mountains of Tunisia, where North Africa's last forest reserves are found. The fact that some of the world's most diverse and least damaged forests are also the homes of indigenous peoples is no accident: the people have utilized but protected them for thousands of years. Many of these areas have recently been seen by others as prime areas to turn into parks or nature preserves. After decades of mostly appalling treatment by outsiders, many indigenous peoples are outraged by this view. They are demanding that their land rights be observed and that they be allowed to control their own lands.

Forests around the world provide a livelihood for many forest people who are not indigenous to them. In Brazil, rubber tappers and Brazil-nut gatherers gain employment from the forest. In Asia and Africa the harvesting of rattan (a climbing palm) provides jobs for tens of thousands of people.

Collecting and cracking open Brazil nuts provides thousands of jobs in the Amazon without destroying the rain forest.

CELLULOSE—BUILDING BLOCKS OF PLANTS AND INDUSTRY

Cellulose is one of the most valuable products derived from trees. After processing, it is powdered and dried and is used as the raw material for many industrial products. These include paper, viscose (a man-made fiber used to make clothing), acetate, and triacetate. Some of the final products made from cellulose include photographic film, eyeglass frames, combs, diapers, toothbrushes, knitting needles, and even car steering wheels. Cellulose is also used as a thickener and binder in products such as paints and toothpaste, and in foods such as fish sticks where it helps to keep the batter from disintegrating.

Paper is the most important product made with cellulose from trees. It currently accounts for 12 percent of all the timber used in the world.

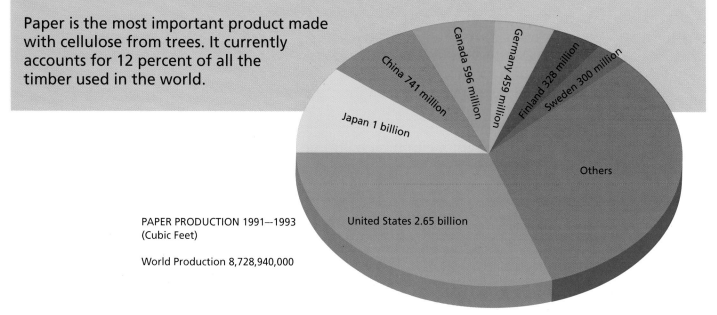

PAPER PRODUCTION 1991--1993
(Cubic Feet)

World Production 8,728,940,000

China 741 million
Canada 596 million
Germany 459 million
Finland 328 million
Sweden 300 million
Japan 1 billion
Others
United States 2.65 billion

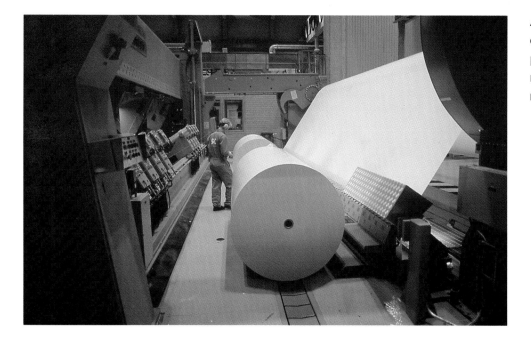

A high-tech Finnish paper mill designed to minimize pollution. In 1993 over 253 million tons of paper were made worldwide.

OTHER FOREST PRODUCTS

Forests are often given a value in terms of the lumber they can produce, but wood is only one of many forest products. The range of other forest products is truly vast and includes foods, fibers, building materials, fuel, medicinal and aromatic plants, gums, and latexes. Forest peoples around the world have used their forests' resources for countless practical purposes—from beautiful clothing made of bark to powerful medicines to cure fevers. And it is the knowledge of forest peoples that has been used in many cases to develop modern consumer goods and medicines.

Rattans—a group of climbing palms—are an example of this. Rattan canes have been used for thousands of years by the peoples of Southeast Asia. Today, furniture and other items made of rattan are worth more than $8 billion every year. Spices like cinnamon and cardamom are also very valuable forest products—now worth over $1 billion annually—that were first used by native peoples. Many of the most expensive perfumes in the world contain ingredients from tropical forest plants, while most of the cheaper scents are made by reacting resin from temperate pine trees with chemicals. Plant products from forests are used in almost every area of our lives. While most of us have chewed gum containing chicle, a sap that is collected from Central American rain forest trees, professional golfers use balls covered in balata latex, another sap that is tapped from the forests of Guyana and Surinam.

Cane furniture made of rattan being taken to market in Thailand

◀ A healing man on Sumba Island in Indonesia uses a forest root called manupeu to treat a sick person.

FORESTS AND WORLD HEALTH

Forests are very important to health. Up to 80 percent of the world's population still rely on traditional medicines, and the ingredients for many of these come directly from trees or plants that grow in forests.

The ancient system of herbal medicine—known as Ayurveda—practiced in India, Sri Lanka, and Southeast Asia uses over 8,000 plant remedies, while traditional Chinese doctors use about 5,000 species of plants. Many of these are found in forests. Indigenous peoples have developed very specialized knowledge of the uses of forest plants. The Kayapo Indians of Brazil, for example, can diagnose and treat over 150 different types of dysentery and diarrhea alone.

But it is not just traditional doctors who use the forests. The active ingredients in many modern medicines are taken directly from forest plants or trees, and others are made in laboratories by copying the chemical structures they contain. A quarter of all the drugs today available by prescription are extracted directly from plants.

Many plant-based drugs are now used to treat illnesses that were once thought incurable. The rosy periwinkle from Madagascar and the Caribbean has given us important drugs that help fight forms of cancer. The use of one of these, vincristine, means that four out of every five children who get leukemia now recover. Active ingredients in the monsoon forest plant known as snake root, or rauwolfia, are very important in controlling high blood pressure and have a tranquilizing effect. An ingredient of the famous Amazonian arrow poison, curare, is now widely used by surgeons as a muscle relaxant.

▲ A researcher checks the dried branches of the Pacific Yew. The chemical, taxol, extracted from this tree has been shown to be effective against various types of cancer.

QUININE AND MALARIA

Quinine—one of the world's most precious medicines—comes from the bark of the cinchona tree, a small, attractive, evergreen with glossy leaves and fragrant flowers. South American Indians first used this bark to treat fevers, and they shared this knowledge with Jesuit missionaries working in Peru nearly 400 years ago. In 1633 Father Calancha, a Jesuit priest, wrote of the "miraculous cures" achieved by drinking a potion made from the powdered bark.

Today, more than 100 million people suffer from the disease malaria, and many of them are treated with quinine. The parasites that cause the disease have become resistant to some of the man-made drugs used to treat it, and quinine is still the most important cure.

When the British ruled India, Europeans who lived there were advised to take quinine in water, as protection against malaria. Flavorings were soon added to improve the bitter taste and the drink became popular. Today, 60 percent of quinine is used medicinally, and the other 40 percent is used in the soft-drink industry in tonic water and other drinks.

A nurse in the children's ward of the malaria hospital in Douala, Cameroon, checks the intravenous connection to an ill child.

Although many pharmaceutical companies are now eager to find new active substances in plants, less than 5 percent of the world's rain forest species have been studied so far for their value to medicine.

Forests can help us to recover from illness and to relax. Recent studies have shown that hospital patients with a view of trees from their windows recover more quickly than those who can see only other buildings. Forests are important as recreation areas as well.

DISAPPEARING FORESTS

A forest plot is cleared in Zaire by cutting down the rain forest trees and then burning the undergrowth. This type of forest clearance is often referred to as "slash-and-burn" agriculture.

Ten thousand years ago forests covered roughly half the land surface on earth. Today, more than one fourth of this forested area has disappeared. Of the remaining forest only one fourth is still undisturbed and is found largely in remote places like northern Canada and Siberia and the Congo and Amazon river basins.

Although people have been clearing forests throughout history, creating areas that have since become barren or desert, most of the damage to forests has occurred in the last 50 years. Half the world's tropical rain forests have been destroyed during the twentieth century. In Central America 90 percent of the rain forest has been destroyed, and only 27,000 sq. mi. (70,000 sq km)—or about 5 percent—of India's original forest cover of more than 580,000 sq. mi. (1.5 million sq km) now remains.

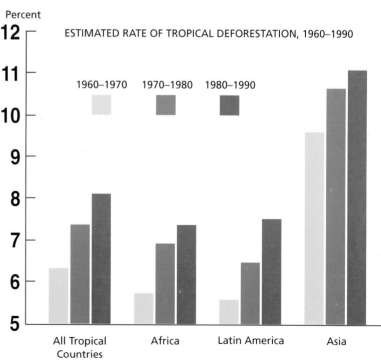

THE CAUSES OF DEFORESTATION

The main causes of the destruction of forests are

- Logging for lumber
- The movement of people into new areas of forest
- The conversion of forests to land for agriculture, ranching, or plantations
- Fuelwood collection
- Atmospheric pollution

12% Pulpwood

27% Sawlogs

7% Other Industrial

54% Fuelwood

Large-scale farming and cattle ranching are estimated to be the main causes of forest destruction in Latin America; uncontrolled logging is the main culprit in Asia and Africa. Many of the world's temperate forests are also being destroyed through logging.

JAPAN'S EFFECT ON WORLD FORESTS

Japan is unusual in the world today since nearly three quarters of its land is covered with pine, cedar, or beech forests, many of which are now in protected areas. Japan is one of only a few countries in the world where forest cover is actually increasing. Yet this one country imports more tropical lumber than the rest of the world combined.

In the 1960s the Philippines was the main supplier of lumber to Japan. Now, most Philippine forests are exhausted. A similar situation arose in Indonesia in the 1970s. By the end of the 1980s Japan had turned its attention elsewhere, and 96 percent of its log imports were coming from Malaysia and Papua New Guinea. In the late 1990s Japan looked farther afield for its lumber, to countries like Brazil and Chile. Indonesian and Korean companies are also buying up large areas of Amazon rain forest.

Pine logs being loaded onto a ship in Miyako, Japan. Japanese forests provide only a tiny proportion of the wood used in Japan: Most is imported.

Nobody is really sure how much forest still remains in the world, but it is thought that forests are being lost at a rate of 1 million acres (400,000 ha) every day. Despite the public outcry in recent years over the destruction of the Amazon rain forest and the pledging in 1990 of more than $500 million by the richest countries of the world to try and save it, Brazilian government figures show that the annual rate of destruction has increased by 34 percent since 1992. A survey carried out by the United Nations Food and Agriculture Organization showed that the rate of global deforestation has doubled since 1980; by 2025 no large areas of tropical forest will be left, apart from those in a few remote parts of Amazonia, Zaire, and Papua New Guinea. Sarawak is currently being deforested faster than anywhere else on Earth, to supply lumber to the Far East. The Solomon Islands are also allowing Asian logging companies to clear-cut most of the islands' forests so fast that they will probably all be gone by about 2006.

Remaining forests

Deforested areas

The demand for tropical lumber has risen 16 times over the last 40 years, but it is the United States, Canada, and the countries of the former Soviet Union that now provide more than half the world's industrial lumber. In both tropical and temperate forests over-logging is not only ruining unique ecosystems and many people's lives, but is threatening the future of the lumber industry as well. The World Bank estimates that of the 33 countries that export tropical lumber today, only 10 will be still in business beyond the year 2000. China, which is now logging the forests of Tibet, is expected to run out of harvestable forests around 2006.

▶ Logging in the Pacific Northwest region of North America. President Collor of Brazil recently pointed out that deforestation occurring in the temperate rain forests of the United States and Canada is just as serious as that occurring in the Amazon.

WASTING WOOD

In many cases forests are destroyed and no use is made of the timber at all. Hydroelectric projects such as the Guri Dam in Venezuela led to the flooding of 1,550 sq. mi. (4,000 sq. km) of unique rain forest. The Balbina Dam in the heart of the Brazilian Amazon caused the flooding of 1 million acres (400,000 ha) of forest. In projects like these useful timber worth millions of dollars was wasted. Cattle ranchers have also been responsible for burning huge areas of forest containing valuable trees such as mahoganies, as well as many other forest products. In North America's temperate rain forests, logging companies have been leaving a quarter of the wood lying on the ground.

SUBSIDIZED DEFORESTATION

Logging in the temperate rain forests of the United States and Canada has been shown to be uneconomic, and it has had to be supported by government subsidies. During the 1980s the North American Forestry Service spent around $40 million of government (taxpayers') money each year, in this way. This meant that American taxpayers were paying millions of dollars to sell some of the world's largest and oldest trees to countries like Japan at a discounted price. At one stage the prices were so artificially low that 400-year-old trees were being sold for less than the cost of a cheeseburger. In Great Britain, subsidies have also encouraged the felling of ancient woodlands and the establishment of large conifer plantations.

Valuable trees killed by flooding caused by the construction of the Samuel Dam in Brazil.

FORESTS AND THE MEAT INDUSTRY

At first glance it is not obvious to see why eating meat might be connected with forest destruction. But in Central America cattle ranching is thought to have caused the loss of two-thirds of the region's forests. Between 1975 and 1995, 90 percent of the beef from animals raised on previously forested land went to the United States, mainly for use in hamburgers. The trade was encouraged because beef could be produced at between a quarter and half the cost of producing it in North America. Brazil is another country in which landowners have been subsidized by their government to cut down or burn forest to create cattle ranches—with disastrous effects.

There are other, less obvious, ways in which forests in developing countries are being destroyed because of the international meat industry. European Union (EU) agricultural policies are part of the problem. A good example is the demand by European countries for cheap pig food, supported by the EU. In Thailand this has led to the destruction of huge areas of tropical rain forest, in order to grow cassava. Cassava starch is turned into tapioca, and this has become a major food for pigs. In Thailand cassava is grown as a cash crop by farmers mainly in the northeast of the country. The area under cultivation has increased from 250,000 acres (100,000 ha) in 1965 to more than ten times that today because of the demand for pig food. The Netherlands alone imports around 44 million tons of tapioca each year. Deforestation of upland areas of Thailand has led to flash floods and hundreds of deaths each year during the 1990s.

Large areas of the Amazon and other rain forests have been cut down to make way for cattle ranches.

Although commercial logging is not the only cause of deforestation, it has caused the degradation of vast areas of rain forest, and the roads built by the logging companies have opened up the forests, enabling settlers to move in.

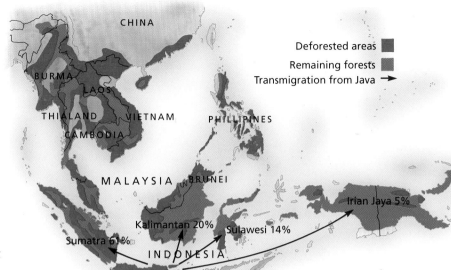

UNFAIR SHARES

Probably the largest cause of deforestation overall is the unequal distribution of wealth and power. The current world economic system encourages individuals and businesses to become as wealthy as they can in as short a time as possible. This means that the rules developed by local communities over very long periods of time in order to protect and manage their environments are now being broken. For example, powerful companies controlled by only a handful of people are able to cause enormous damage to forests and to push out local people, without really being challenged. But large numbers of poor people are also moving into rain forests and cutting down plots because they have been forced or obliged to move from other areas.

In Indonesia, an estimated one million families who have been relocated as part of the country's controversial transmigration program are each clearing more than an acre (0.4 ha) of new forest every year. That is because rain forest soils are generally too poor to support cultivation for more than a few years. When families find good agricultural land they are often forced off by powerful landowners. This is particularly true in Brazil, where 4.5 percent of the landowners own 81 percent of all farmland, and 70 percent of rural families have no land at all.

▼ People who have been moved from the overcrowded island of Sumatra to outlying islands as part of the Indonesian government's transmigration program have cut down rain forest to grow rice and other crops.

29

Many tropical countries now have enormous debts to institutions such as the World Bank, which lend money for "development projects." Because of their debts, these countries are under pressure to cut down their forests in order to try to make as much money as they can. This may be through selling the timber, constructing dams that will generate hydroelectric power or through plantation agriculture such as the cultivation of African oil palm (grown for oil that is used in many foods, soap, and cosmetics). Foreign aid in the form of money or expertise from abroad that is given to less wealthy countries has also led to forest loss. In some cases loans to developing countries, such as Guyana, have been made only on the understanding that foreign companies will be allowed to come and exploit the timber.

DISAPPEARING FORESTS IN SCANDINAVIA
Sweden and Finland are two countries that are thought by many to be models of good forest management. Sweden has 58 percent of its land covered in forests, and Finland has nearly 70 percent. In both countries forest cover is rising. However, this has hidden the fact that a wildlife crisis has developed in Scandinavia.

An aerial view of a large African oil palm plantation and the workers' accommodation in southwest Cameroon.

In Finland only about 3 percent of the ancient "old-growth" forests remain. These forests are the last refuges of rare European plants and animals such as moose, bear, lynx, wolves, and wolverine. Until recently the forests on the mountains in northern Scandinavia remained relatively untouched. Now they are scheduled to be cut down. Foresters in both countries say, quite correctly, that several trees are planted for each one cut down. But the replacement forests typically consist of a single tree species, such as lodgepole pine or spruce, which cannot support the same variety of wildlife.

In Sweden it is not only plant and animal species that are facing extinction because of the destruction of the ancient forests: an ancient way of life is also under threat. The nomadic Saami, or Lapps, of Sweden have used the northern forests for centuries, spending the winters there with their herds of reindeer. The new plantation forests do not support the lichens that the reindeer need to eat to survive the winter. At the same time, some logging companies regard reindeer as pests and are trying to exclude the Saami by law.

For hundreds of years, Saami people and their reindeer herds have relied on the wild forests in northern Scandinavia during the winter months.

THE FUELWOOD CRISIS

Throughout the world, more than 2 billion people rely on fuelwood for cooking or heating. As more trees are cut down, wood is becoming increasingly scarce across large parts of sub-Saharan Africa, the Middle East, and Asia. Today more than 100 million people are unable to find enough fuelwood for even their most basic energy needs.

In many developing countries fuelwood accounts for a large proportion of all energy consumption. More than 90 percent of the energy used in countries such as Burkina Faso, Tanzania, Nepal, and Ethiopia comes from wood. Wood even provides oil-rich Nigeria with 80 percent of its energy needs.

In the foothills of Nepal, women now have to spend a day collecting the firewood that their mothers would have been able to collect in just one hour. Keeping home fires lighted in parts of Nepal and Tanzania now takes 230 person days per family per year. Families in Ougadougou in Burkina Faso and Port au Prince in Haiti spend as much as 30 percent of their income on fuelwood.

A young girl in Kathmandu, Nepal, carries a basket of firewood to market.

FOREST DEATH

Atmospheric pollution has been having a serious effect on forests in many parts of the world. In the early 1980s some European forests began to suffer from what came to be known as *Waldsterben*, which means "forest death" in German. Germany was the first country to become affected, and more than half of the forests there are now suffering. Nearly 200,000 sq. mi. (500,000 sq. km) of forests in 19 European countries are also dying. The problem, however, is not restricted to Europe: it is now affecting forests in 37 out of 50 U.S. states, in China, and in nearly 2.5 million acres (1 million ha) of the former Soviet Union.

Scientists have identified more than 180 possible causes, ranging from errors in the way the trees were planted to acid rain and climate change. It is now generally agreed that the cause is the combined effect of pollutants such as ozone from car exhausts and acid rain from the burning of fossil fuels, together with other factors.

When there is less wood for people to use, they begin to economize. Some families in developing nations no longer have enough wood to boil their drinking water, which means that they are more likely to catch water-borne diseases. In some areas people gather animal dung to burn as fuel, but this has the effect of removing what would otherwise have been an important source of fertilizer from the soil. Every year, Asians and Africans burn enough dung to grow 20 million tons of grain.

▼ Air pollution has been partly responsible for the death of forests near industrial areas. This scene is near Port Talbot in Wales.

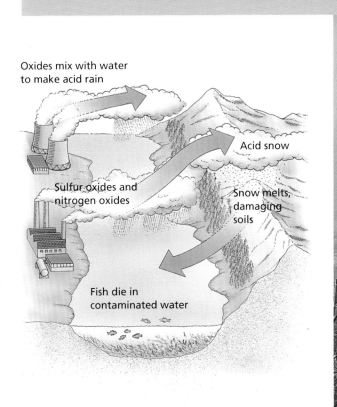

Oxides mix with water to make acid rain

Acid snow

Sulfur oxides and nitrogen oxides

Snow melts, damaging soils

Fish die in contaminated water

WHAT IS BEING DONE?

A round the world many people are very concerned about what is happening to forests. Countless individuals, environmental groups, and some governments are trying to find ways to protect and manage forests for the future.

There are many different issues involved in saving forests, and different actions are needed in different places. Where large-scale destructive logging is going on, major changes in attitude are needed now, from governments, international organizations, and multinational companies. Unfortunately, many governments—such as those of Guyana, Guinea, and the Solomon Islands—are still encouraging the logging of their forests because of the huge sums of money that they and the logging companies will make from selling the timber.

Mayan people in Belize protesting the logging of rain forest by a multinational company in south Toledo

However, other governments, such as that of Great Britain, and some powerful organizations, like the World Bank, now accept that the rate of forest loss is a serious problem and that some of their policies and funding have led to an increase in forest destruction. Many conservationists believe that there should be a complete and immediate ban on the logging of all "ancient growth" forests and suggest that this may even mean paying companies for not logging certain areas.

REFORESTING VIETNAM

The Vietnam War, which ended in 1975, left 8,500 sq. mi. (22,000 sq. km) of forest destroyed or seriously damaged. In 1986, Vietnam began its National Conservation Strategy, which aims to regrow large areas of the country's forests. The plan is to plant at least 500 million trees a year in the hope that forest cover will return to about 50 percent of the country. Tree planting has become one of the official activities of Vietnamese schoolchildren, and every pupil must not only plant a tree, but also take care of it.

People planting new trees in north Vietnam in an effort to repair the damage caused during the Vietnam War and by excessive logging.

SUSTAINABLE FORESTS

The key issues of forest conservation revolve around sustainability —using forests and the animals and plants that live in them, in ways that do not permanently damage them. This means cutting only as much timber or other products as the forests can support so that they will continue to be productive in future years. It also means respecting people who have traditional rights to forests.

CHARCOAL, COPPICING, AND CONSERVATION

Currently 95 percent of all charcoal used in Great Britain is imported. The wood can come from anywhere, but is mainly from tropical forests, including the mangrove forests of Southeast Asia and the rain forests of South America. In Great Britain, however, there has been a long tradition of making charcoal from British wood, which only began to die out 50 years ago.

Today, British forests are once again starting to produce charcoal, using the traditional, sustainable system of woodland management called "coppicing." Many different sorts of trees are used, including ash, hazel, oak, sweet chestnut, and hornbeam. In this system trees are cut to the ground, but new stems quickly grow back and are harvested at 15-year intervals. Harvesting the forest in this way provides a range of wildlife habitats and encourages wildflowers and butterflies.

It has been calculated that Great Britain's broadleaved woodlands are growing about 2.4 million tons of hardwood each year, but only a third of this is harvested. Since it takes 6 tons of wood to make each ton of charcoal, all the charcoal that Great Britain needs could be made by using just 15 percent of what is currently going to waste.

The wealthy countries of the world must try to reduce their consumption of forest products in general and increase the use of recycled materials such as paper and cardboard. In the United States more than half of all the paper used is used for packaging, and it is estimated that in under 50 years three billion trees will be needed each year just to supply toilet paper to the world's population.

The use of more wood from plantations will help save ancient forests and also the millions of species of plants and animals that live in them. Many forest species are now threatened with extinction, and environmental groups are pressing for bans on the national and international trade in them.

Hundreds of different products are now made out of recycled paper. These include newspapers, packaging, and envelopes.

PROTECTED AREAS

Like the animals that live in them, only a tiny proportion of the world's remaining forests have any legal protection. Environmental organizations such as the World Wildlife Fund (WWF) and Friends of the Earth are trying to help save forests by campaigning for their urgent protection. They are also helping to inform governments and the public about the rates of destruction and possible effects of forest loss. WWF has called for the setting up of more protected areas and is campaigning for 10 percent of the world's forests to be protected by the year 2000.

People protesting to protect an area of rain forest in Hawaii

For millions of indigenous people, sustainable forest use has been central to their cultures for thousands of years, and it is no accident that many of the surviving areas of intact forest are or were until recently their homes. Traditional forest peoples want their rights to their lands guaranteed so that they can manage areas in their own ways. They do not want their traditional lands turned into parks from which they may then be excluded or to be told by others how to manage their affairs.

NEW OPPORTUNITIES IN LATVIA

Latvia is one of the Baltic countries that used to be part of the Soviet Union. Nearly half the country is forested, and lumber is its main export. At present logging companies are clear-cutting Latvian forests—under strict orders from the State Forestry Service. Most of the companies would prefer to leave dead and overaged trees to provide habitats for owls, woodpeckers, and insects. They would rather leave the forests in swampy areas—that have little timber value—to beavers and other wildlife. They know that clearing all the small trees, as they are obliged to do under Latvian law, actually costs them money.

Things are beginning to change. In the 37,000-acre (15,000-ha) territory of Melzole, a forestry project has been set up in which the normal forestry rules don't apply. Foresters are not being forced to cut down every tree, and wildlife and trees have benefited. In one 11-acre (4.5-ha) plot there has been an estimated saving of over $1,000 by leaving some trees standing.

If the Latvian government encourages all the lumber companies to work in this more environmentally sensitive, and more cost-effective, way the future will be brighter for the forests, for wildlife such as wolves, elk, and black stork, and for the foresters themselves.

Nearly half of Latvia is forested, but logging companies have the capacity to clear-cut most of Latvia in 10–20 years if the forests are not managed sustainably.

A Mexican child reads about World Environment Day at a school in a remote village surrounded by mangrove forest in the Yucatan Peninsula.

A ROLE FOR EVERYONE

In summary, there are a number of important ways of conserving forests, and the most important of these are action by local governments, multinational organizations, and companies to ban uncontrolled logging; the sustainable use of forests; reducing our consumption of forest products in general; increasing the use of plantation products and recycled materials; respecting the rights of indigenous peoples; creating properly protected areas; introducing and enforcing bans on the trade in rare species; and reducing air pollution.

Individuals can also help slow forest loss by using more recycled things—paper, toilet paper, and paper towels, for example—and by buying ecolabeled products (see box on facing page) wherever possible. We can also help by trying to pollute the environment less—for example, by not using the car so often and by trying to travel by public transportation—and by planting trees locally.

ECOLABELING

At present it is not clear where much of the wood we use has come from or whether a door or toilet seat is made from a tree that was illegally felled. The idea behind ecolabeling is to enable people to see where the wood products we use have come from. Under this plan, all products that come from well-managed forests carry a label that shows this. This would enable people to choose which to buy and thus help support the sustainable use of forests.

The Forest Stewardship Council (FSC) was set up in 1993 to provide a way of checking where timber comes from and how it has been harvested. Under the plan, forests around the world are visited and assessed. If they are producing timber in a way that is sustainable for the forseeable future and meet other social and environmental criteria, they become "certified" and receive the FSC stamp of approval. To meet the FSC standard, forests must be managed to make sure that

● The harvest of all products (whether wood or products such as nuts or fibers) can be sustained, that soils and water will be protected, and that the forest's contribution to local weather and global climate patterns remains unchanged.

● The original variety of plants, animals, and other organisms depending on the forest can be maintained.

● Indigenous people, forestry employees, and local communities benefit, as well as the local and national economies.

● A number of forests have already been certified in Great Britain, Papua New Guinea, the United States, Poland, South Africa, Zimbabwe, and Mexico. When products from these forests go on sale they display the FSC logo, and consumers can be assured that they are helping ensure the long-term future of forests.

A Mexican holds a plank from a forest that has recently been certified. This means the local people have a plan to cut timber and protect the forest for the future.

The FSC logo is used to enable people to choose products made from wood that has come from well-managed forests.

WHAT CAN WE DO?

The scale of deforestation is so great that many people think there is little they can do to help save our forests. Yet ordinary people working together can be powerful. Whereas politicians and governments tend to think only a few years ahead, public opinion is often more farsighted. Many people are worried about the effects of deforestation on future generations. In the past, public opinion has helped change the law on hunting whales, on the protection of Antarctica, and on lead in gasoline. So what people think—and do—*can* have a real effect on how the world's forests are used.

A Cub Scout in the United States gathering old newspapers for recycling.

THINGS YOU CAN DO

- Become aware of the issues concerning the use of forests.

- Encourage your school, office, and parents to use more recycled products.

- Try to consume less. For example, you might avoid buying products with excessive packaging.

- Try to pollute the environment less. One way to do this is to use cars less and bicycles and public transportation more. Air pollution kills forests and contributes to global warming.

- Join an environmental group, such as WWF or Friends of the Earth.

- Find out about tree-planting programs in your area, and take part.

- Write to your government representative and ask what his or her party's policy is on forests, recycling, and conservation—and tell him or her what you think about these issues.

The use of public transportation in countries like Denmark helps reduce the atmospheric pollution that is killing European forests.

A volunteer in Australia planting and watering a tree seedling

PUBLIC OPINION AND THE WORLD BANK

The World Bank lends large sums of money to governments for development projects around the world. However, it has often faced strong criticism because of the severe environmental and social effects of some of the projects it has funded. In one case, the World Bank loaned money to Ivory Coast and Ghana in Africa to open up the countries' last remaining natural forest to large-scale logging. However, the bank did not ask for guarantees that the forest would be managed sustainably.

Because of this, WWF and Friends of the Earth organized a card-writing campaign in Great Britain to try to change the World Bank's forest policy. Over 30,000 cards were sent to Members of Parliament. As a result of this, and similar campaigns in other countries, the World Bank was forced to adopt a new policy stating that it "will under no circumstances finance commercial logging in primary tropical moist forests."

FORESTS FOR THE FUTURE

The world's forests are disappearing quickly, especially in the tropics. If current trends continue, in 50 years only small patches of tropical rain forest will survive, and most of the world's remaining forests will be in the temperate and boreal regions of North America, Scandinavia, and Siberia. Some scientists fear that we are on the brink of a global environmental catastrophe. It is almost too late, but there is just time if action is taken quickly.

As we have seen, there are many things that can be done by us as individuals, by our governments, and by large companies to save the world's forests. The responsibility for stopping large-scale destruction lies mainly with the governments and citizens of the rich nations. It is the demand for forest products for non-essential uses such as excessive packaging that has helped destroy many forests. As individuals we can consume less, recycle more, buy goods from sustainably managed forests, join environmental pressure groups, and campaign for our governments and businesses to act more responsibly. Governments and international organizations must take action to protect areas of natural old-growth forest throughout the world. This may include signing international agreements prohibiting the trade in tree species that are near extinction and in wood that does not come from properly managed forests.

Temperate forest still covers much of the French and Spanish Pyrenees and is protected within national parks.

Protecting forests is not just a question of money. In 1990 representatives of the seven wealthiest nations, known as the G7, reached an agreement to pledge up to $500 million to combat the destruction of the Amazon rain forest. The latest satellite information from Brazil, in 1996, has shown that the rate of destruction has increased by 34 percent since 1992. What is needed is a fundamental change in the lifestyles of the people of the rich nations. Some people may object to this, but it is a small price to pay to protect the future of the forests—and the planet.

At present it is the people in the developing nations—who rely on forests for their immediate needs—who are losing out. For them the loss of forest does not mean simply paying more for products or using less paper, it is a matter of life or death.

The challenge is to protect the world's forests in ways that keep the planet's life-support system in working order while continuing to satisfy the basic human needs for housing, warmth, clean water, and fresh air. This is not an easy task, but if governments, individuals, and environmental groups work toward a common goal of halting and reversing the loss and degradation of all types of woodland, then the outlook for the twenty-first century will be brighter.

Prospectors and mining companies have caused destruction of large areas of the Amazon rain forests. In many cases the rain forest trees are cut down to make charcoal to smelt the metal ores.

GLOSSARY

AROMATIC PLANTS Plants that contain substances with strong aromas (smells), often used to make perfumes.

BOREAL Northern.

CONIFER An evergreen tree that usually has cones.

CONSERVATIONIST A person who believes that nature should be protected.

COPPICING A forestry system where trees are cut in such a way that new poles grow from the stumps and are harvested every 15–20 years.

CANOPY The uppermost layer of branches formed by a tree or trees.

DECIDUOUS FOREST A forest containing trees that shed their leaves each year.

DEFORESTATION The removal of trees from an area.

ECOLABEL A label providing information about where a particular product has come from and relevant environmental details.

ECOSYSTEM A community of animals and plants and the environment they live in.

EVERGREEN A description of trees that keep their leaves all year round. The opposite of deciduous.

FLOODED FOREST An area of forest that is flooded permanently or at certain times of the year.

GLOBAL WARMING The gradual warming up of the surface of the planet as a result of a change in the composition of atmospheric gases, especially an increase in the percentage of carbon dioxide.

HABITAT The natural home of a particular plant or animal.

INDIGENOUS Belonging originally or naturally to a particular place.

LATEX A milky sap that is produced by various plants and trees.

MANGROVE FOREST Evergreen forests found along some tropical coastlines. The trees have special roots that stick up from the mud and can take in oxygen.

MONTANE FOREST Forest that occurs above 3,000 ft. (900 m).

MULTINATIONAL COMPANIES Large companies that operate on a global scale.

NOMADIC Describes people who do not have any one home location but move regularly from place to place.

PLANTATION An area in which a single crop is planted, often in rows.

RAIN FOREST A forest that has high rainfall all year round.

RECYCLED MATERIAL Materials that are made from waste. For example, paper made from waste paper.

SUSTAINABLE USE A way of using resources that does not threaten their long-term survival or the survival of the plants and animals, including humans, that depend on them.

TEMPERATE Mild or moderate.

TRANSMIGRATION The relocation often of tens of thousands of people from their homeland to another location.

TROPICS The area characterized by high temperatures and rainfall that lies between the tropics of Capricorn and Cancer.

FURTHER INFORMATION

ADDRESSES TO WRITE TO

Friends of the Earth
1025 Vermont Avenue NW
Suite 300
Washington, D.C. 20005-6303
(202) 783-7400

Reforest the Earth
2218 Blossomwood Court NW
Olympia, WA 98502

Earth Living Foundation
P.O. Box 188
Hesperus, CO 81326
(970) 385-5500

The World Rainforest Movement
Chapel Row
Chadlington
Oxfordshire OX7 3NA
Tel: 01608 676691

World Wildlife Fund
1250 24th Street NW
P.O. Box 96555
Washington, D.C. 20077-7795

Survival International
11–15 Emerald Street
London WC1N 3QL
Tel: 0171 242 1441

Forest Stewardship Council
RD 1 Box 182
Waterbury, VT 05676
(800) 244-6257

National Arbor Day Foundation
100 Arbor Avenue
Nebraska City, NE 68410
(402) 474-5655

BOOKS TO READ

Anderson, Robert. *Forests: Identifying Propaganda Techniques.* (Opposing Viewpoints Juniors.) Greenhaven, 1992.

Bash, Barbara. *Ancient Ones: The World of the Old-Growth Douglas Fir.* San Francisco: Sierra Club Books, 1994.

Challand, Helen J. *Vanishing Forests.* (Saving Planet Earth.) Danbury, CT: Children's Press, 1991.

Gallant, Roy A. *Vanishing Forests.* New York: Simon & Schuster Children's Books, 1992.

Ganeri, Anita. *Forests.* (Habitats.) Austin, TX: Raintree Steck-Vaughn, 1997.

Goldstein, Natalie. *Rebuilding Prairies and Forests.* (Restoring Nature.) Danbury, CT: Children's Press, 1994.

Goodman, Billy. *The Rain Forest.* (Planet Earth.) Boston: Little Brown, 1992.

Leggett, Jeremy. *Dying Forests.* Tarrytown, NY: Marshall Cavendish, 1991.

Lewington, Anna. *Atlas of Rain Forests.* Austin, TX: Raintree Steck-Vaughn, 1997.

Morrison, Marion. *The Amazon Rain Forest and Its People.* (People and Places.) Austin, TX: Raintree Steck-Vaughn, 1993.

Sadler, Tony. *Forests and Their Environment.* (Science and Our Future.) New York: Cambridge University Press, 1994.

Sayre, April P. *Temperate Deciduous Forest.* (Exploring Earth's Biomes.) New York: 21st Century Books, 1994.

Sayre, April P. *Tropical Rainforest.* (Exploring Earth's Biomes.) New York: 21st Century Books, 1994.

Tangley, Laura. *The Rainforest.* (Earth At Risk.) New York: Chelsea House, 1992.

INDEX

Numbers that appear in **bold** refer to pictures as well as text.

Amazon region 19, 24, 26, 27, 45
Australia **43**

biodiversity 12
boreal forests 6, 7, 15
  trees **7**

Canada 24
carbon dioxide 14
Caribbean region 22
cattle ranching 25, **28**
Central America 24
  Belize **34**
charcoal 37
chicle 21
conifers 7

deciduous trees 7
deforestation
  causes 25, 27, 28, 32–33
  effects of **10**, **11**, 14, **15**, **45**
  flooding 11
  government subsidies 27
  rate of **24**, 26
Denmark **36**, **43**

ecosystems 4, 26

Finland 20, 30
foods 4, 19
Forest Stewardship Council 41
fuelwood 17, 25, 32–33

global warming 14
greenhouse effect **14**

housing **16**
hydroelectric projects **27**

Indonesia 22
Industrial Revolution 17

Japan **25**

Kayapo 22

latex 21
Latvia 39
logging **5**, 25, 29, 34

Madagascar **15**, 22
mangroves **13**
medicines 10, 17, 21, 22–23
  curare 22
  quinine 22
  vincristine 22

nature preserves/parks 19, 38
Nenets (herders) **18**
Nepal **32**
New Zealand **16**, **36**

Penan (tribespeople) **17**
plantations 6, 30
pollution, effect 33
primary forest 6
products of forests **21**
  Brazil nuts **19**
  cellulose 20
  furniture **21**
  paper 5, **20**
  spices 21

rain forest
  temperate **8**, 19
  tropical **9**, **13**, **14**, **17**, **26**
  trees 9
recycling 37, 40, **42**
rubber tappers 19

Scandinavia 30, 31, 44
secondary forest 6
Siberia 18, 24
slash-and-burn farming **24**
South Africa 9
subarctic forest *see boreal forest*
Sweden 31

temperate forest 5, 7, 8, 44
  trees **8**
Tibet 26
Tlingit 19
tropical forest 7, **9**, **13**, **14**

United States 5, **42**
  Alaska 19
  Baker National Park,
    Washington 6
  Hawaii **38**

Vietnam, reforestation 35

water 4
World Bank 35, 43
World Wildlife Fund 38, 43

PICTURE ACKNOWLEDGMENTS

Bruce Coleman Collection 9 (Luiz Claudio Marigo), 15 (Konrad Wothe), 22 top (Alain Compost); Bryan and Cherry Alexander 18 (Edward Parker), 31; Forlaget Flachs 36 inset (Ole Steen Hansen), 37 (Dieter Betz), 43 (Svend Erik Andersen); Hedgehog House 16 (Colin Monteath), 36 (Lynda Harper); Oxford Scientific Films 24 (Martyn Colbeck), 43 (Bob Goodale); Edward Parker 39, 40, 41; Science Photo Library *cover background* (NASA), 8 (Simon Fraser), 14 (Dr Morley Read), 22 bottom (Philippe Plailly/Eurelios), 33 (Simon Fraser); Still Pictures 4 (Alain Compost), 10 (Nigel Dickinson), 11 (Mark Edwards), 13 (Bojan Brecelj), 17 right (Dario Novellino), 19 (Mark Edwards), 20 (Mark Edwards), 21 (Mark Edwards), 23 (Mark Edwards), 25 (Jonathan Kaplan), 27 (John Maier), 28 (Mark Edwards), 29 (Paul Harrison), 30 (Edward Parker), 32 (Jorgen Schytte), 34 (Nigel Dickinson), 35 (Heldur Netocny), 44 (Georges Lopez), 45 (Mark Edwards); Tony Stone Images 5 (Vince Streano), 6 (Brett Baunton), 12 (Daniel J Cox), 26 (Zigy Kalunzy), 38 (G Brad Lewis), 42 (Bruce Forster); Wayland Picture Library 17 left; Zefa *front cover*.
All artwork is by Peter Bull, except the book icons used on page 1, the contents page and chapter headings, which are by Tina Barber.